Alphabet Books

Weather

ABC

An Alphabet Book

by B. A. Hoena

Consulting Editor: Gail Saunders-Smith, PhD

Capstone press

Mankato, Minnesota

A is for above.

Look at the sky above. Do you see clouds or sunshine? Sometimes you can tell what the weather will be like just by looking up.

B is for blizzard.

Where did everything go? There was
a blizzard. During the storm, this car
was buried in snow.

C is for clouds.

Not all clouds bring rain. Small, puffy cumulus clouds are a sign that it could be a nice day.

4

D is for downpour.

Oh no, it's a downpour! Lots of rain falls when dark thunderstorm clouds float overhead.

5

E is for earmuffs.

If you don't have a hat, then earmuffs will do. On cold winter days, you need warm clothes to go outside and play.

6

F is for fog.

Fog forms when wet, warm air cools. Be careful. Fog makes it difficult to see what's around you.

G is for rain gauge.

Not sure how how much rain fell during a storm? A rain gauge measures the rain for you.

H is for hail.

Hail forms in thunderstorm clouds, where the air is cool. These chunks of ice and snow sometimes fall to the ground during storms.

9

I is for icicle.

The sun is shining, and the snow is melting. But it's still cold outside. Water from the melted snow freezes as it drips, forming icicles.

J is for jacket.

When the weather is chilly,
put on your jacket. Zip up,
and it'll keep you warm
if there's a cool breeze.

K is for kite.

Windy days are good kite-flying weather.
Let out some string. The wind will lift
your kite higher and higher.

L is for lightning.

During thunderstorms, lightning streaks across the sky, lighting up the night. Then . . . **KA-BOOM!**

13

M is for meteorologist.

What will the weather be like? Turn on the news. A meteorologist will tell you if the weather will be sunny or cloudy.

72

76

87

83

90

N is for numbers.

The numbers on a thermometer tell you the temperature. As it gets hotter outside, the number gets bigger.

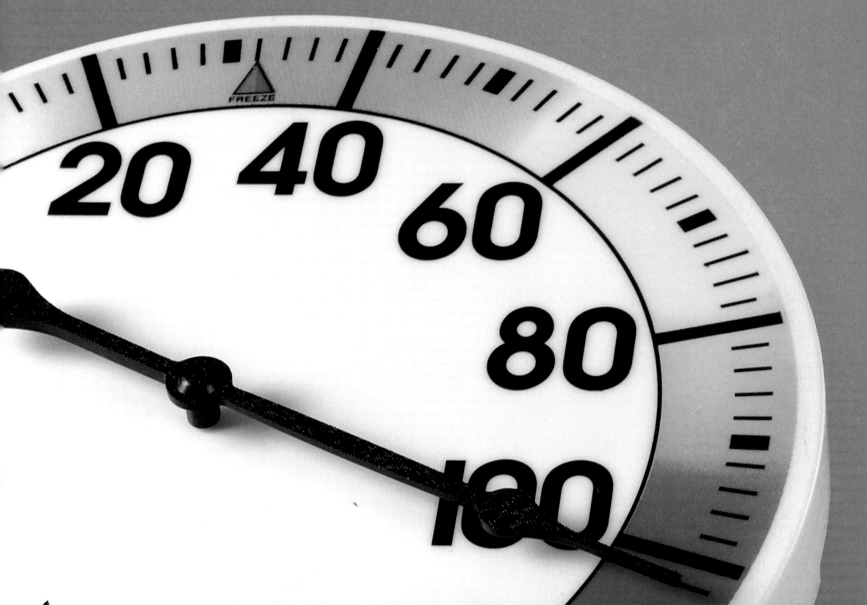

O is for overcast.

On overcast days, gray stratus clouds fill the sky. A light rain might fall from these flat, low-flying clouds.

P is for puddle.

Rain gathers in puddles. Put on your rain boots and jump on in. Puddles are like swimming pools for your feet.

17

Q is for quiet.

It's a quiet, relaxing day. The lake looks as smooth as glass because there's no wind or rain.

18

R is for rainbow.

Rain can create a beautiful show. You see a rainbow when sunlight shines through water droplets in the air.

S is for snow.

Winter weather can be cold,
but it's still fun to play outside.
You can make angels in the snow.

T is for tornado.

Look out! It's a twister! Strong winds are whirling and swirling about, causing a tornado.

U is for umbrella.

The weather is rainy, but you don't have to stay inside. Grab an umbrella. It'll keep you dry.

V is for weather vane.

Which way is the wind blowing?
Look up at a weather vane
if you want to know.

W is for wind.

The wind is blowing, tossing your hair about. Wind is the flow of cold and warm air moving around.

X is for extremely dry.

The land is extremely dry and cracked.
This area has been without rain
for a long time. There's been a drought.

25

Y is for year.

Weather changes throughout the year.
Spring rain helps flowers grow. Summer
is sunny. Leaves change colors in fall.
Winter can be snowy and cold.

Z is for zero.

The thermometer says zero degrees. It's freezing cold. Put on your hat and coat if you want to play in the snow.

Fun Facts about Weather

Hail can be as large as a softball.

The hottest recorded temperature in the United States was 134 degrees Fahrenheit (56.7 degrees Celsius) in Death Valley, California, on July 10, 1913.

The temperature inside a lightning bolt is hotter than the surface of the sun.

About 100,000 thunderstorms occur each year in the United States.

About 1,000 lightning bolts strike the earth every second.

Clouds are made of very tiny water droplets. It takes about 1 million cloud droplets to make 1 raindrop.

The fastest tornado winds recorded were 286 miles (460 kilometers) an hour in Wichita Falls, Texas, on April 2, 1958.

The coldest recorded temperature in the United States was minus 79.8 degrees Fahrenheit (minus 62.1 degrees Celsius), in Prospect Creek, Alaska, on January 23, 1971.

Glossary

cumulus cloud (KYOO-myoo-luhss KLOUD)—a white, puffy cloud with a flat, rounded base

degree (di-GREE)—a unit for measuring temperature

drought (DROUT)—a long spell of very dry weather

gauge (GAYJ)—an instrument used for measuring; a rain gauge shows how much rain has fallen.

meteorologist (MEE-tee-ur-AWL-uh-jist)—a person who studies and predicts the weather

stratus cloud (STRA-tuhss KLOUD)—a low cloud that forms over a large area; stratus clouds often bring light rain.

thermometer (thur-MOM-uh-tur)—an instrument used to measure temperature

Read More

Eckart, Edana. *Watching the Weather.* Watching Nature. New York: Children's Press, 2004.

Granowsky, Alvin. *Rain or Shine.* My World. Brookfield, Conn.: Copper Beech Books, 2001.

Orme, Helen. *What Makes Weather?* What? Where? Why? Milwaukee: Gareth Stevens, 2004.

Internet Sites

FactHound offers a safe, fun way to find Internet sites related to this book. All of the sites on FactHound have been researched by our staff.

Here's how:
1. Visit *www.facthound.com*
2. Type in this special code **0736836675** for age-appropriate sites. Or enter a search word related to this book for a more general search.
3. Click on the **Fetch It** button.

FactHound will fetch the best sites for you!

Index

A+ Books are published by Capstone Press,
151 Good Counsel Drive, P.O. Box 669, Mankato, Minnesota 56002.
www.capstonepress.com

1 2 3 4 5 6 10 09 08 07 06 05

Library of Congress Cataloging-in-Publication Data
Hoena, B. A.
    Weather ABC: An Alphabet Book / by B. A. Hoena.
    p. cm.—(A+ Books. Alphabet Books)
    Includes bibliographical references and index.
    ISBN 0-7368-3667-5 (hardcover)
    1. Weather—Juvenile literature. 2. English language—Alphabet—Juvenile literature. I. Title.
II. Series.
QC981.3.H64 2005
428.1'3—dc22   2004015234

Summary: Introduces weather through photographs and brief text that uses one word relating
    to weather for each letter of the alphabet.

Credits
Amanda Doering, editor; Heather Kindseth, set designer; Jenny Bergstrom, book designer;
    Kelly Garvin, photo researcher; Scott Thoms, photo editor

Photo Credits
Bruce Coleman Inc./Atlantide, 4; Bruce Coleman Inc./David Ortiz, 23; Bruce Coleman Inc./Julie
Eggers, 7; Bruce Coleman Inc./Rex Butcher, 26 (maple leaves); Capstone Press/Gary Sundermeyer,
12; Capstone Press/Karon Dubke, 6, 8, 11, 14, 15, 22, 24; Color-Pic, Inc./Susan E. Degginger, 18;
Corbis, 29; Corbis/A & J Verkaik, cover, 13; Corbis/Craig Tuttle, 26 (pinecone); Corbis/Jim
Craigmyle, 27; Corbis/Jim Reed, 21; Corbis/John M. Roberts, 26 (tulips); Corbis/JS Productions,
19; Corbis/Julie Habel, 20; Corbis/Roy Morsch, 5; Getty Images Inc./Burgess Blevins, 2;
Houserstock/Steve Bly, 10; Index Stock Imagery/Diaphor Agency, 3; Ingram Publishing, 1;
Mira/Ted Russell, 25; OneBlueShoe, 16; Photodisc, 26 (sunflower), 28 (both); SuperStock/Mike
Ford, 17; UNICORN Stock Photos/Patti McConville, 9

Note to Parents, Teachers, and Librarians
Weather ABC: An Alphabet Book uses colorful photographs and a nonfiction format to
introduce children to characteristics about weather while building a mastery of the
alphabet. This book is designed to be read independently by an early reader or to be
read aloud to a pre-reader. The images help early readers and listeners understand the
text and concepts discussed. The book encourages further learning by including the
following sections: Fun Facts about Weather, Glossary, Read More, Internet Sites, and
Index. Early readers may need assistance using these features.